WHITE RACIALISM

AND

AMERICAN NATIONALISM

BENJAMIN GARLAND

Dedicated to all of the right wing political prisoners and dissidents who are sitting in jail or awaiting trial right now for daring to stand against the destruction of America and its history.

Author's Note

The following consists of four articles I wrote for Daily Stormer during 2017 and 2018, wherein I make the case for the legitimacy of racially based nationalism among white American patriots.

They were written in the context of an ongoing debate about which direction the pro-white struggle in America should take. As a result, I almost immediately regretted mixing in the "movement" drama, fearing that this would cause the articles to become dated very quickly.

Because of this, I considered rewriting them. However, upon re-reading the articles, I decided that they actually stand on their own pretty well. Even if you, the reader, are far removed from the environment that initially spawned them, I believe the articles will still be coherent, therefore I have decided to leave them as is, as they were originally written.

I hope that you don't find any of it confusing and if you do, I apologize.

What is contained in this book may also shock and enrage you, or it may not. That all depends on your political views, preconceived ideas and personal sensibilities. What I hope is that it will at least intrigue and entertain you. It is one part polemic, one part intellectual argument and one part history lesson, written in the spirit of maximum political incorrectness, with the goal of packing a punch.

I received much positive feedback from the articles when they were originally published (and some negative) and they sparked quite a bit of interesting and heated debate, which tells me I did my job correctly.

Even the anti-American, anti-free speech Jewish Anti-Defamation League did a write-up on them, which was quite the honor.[*]

The reader is invited to send any questions, comments, love letters, insults or hate mail to the author at theendofzion02@gmail.com

Enjoy!

– Ben Garland, January 12, 2019

---

[*] https://www.adl.org/resources/backgrounders/daily-stormer-book-clubs-sbc

Contents

The Alt-Right Represents True American Nationalism

I can almost hear the snickers and jeers over the title of this article, from left and right alike.

For those who think the idea that the Alt-Right is the only true representative of American Nationalism is far-fetched, here is my challenge to you:

Show me where I am wrong.

Show me how the Founding Fathers weren't race realists.

Show me how America wasn't a White Patriarchy prior to 1920.

Show me where the Founding Fathers said women should have the right to vote.

Show me where the Founding Fathers said blacks should have full citizenship.

It's really rather simple:

We, the Alt-Right, are White Nationalists, and we want to reinstate the Patriarchy.

America was founded – in the words of the ever-insightful Fash McQueen – as "a moral, patriarchal, limited-franchise Republic – A White Ethno-State."

The traditional family was seen as the backbone of the nation and was revered above all else.

Women were considered property. They were taught to obey their husbands and that their world was exclusively home, hearth, and family. They were not to hold office, vote or mix in the meetings of men or public affairs in any capacity. Sluttery was seen as an unforgivable sin.

Women were cherished for this; they were not oppressed. In fact – without any room for debate –

they were much happier back then when they were fulfilling this sacred and natural role than they are now after having allegedly been "liberated."

Here are a few quotes from the most important and celebrated Founding Father of all, Thomas Jefferson:

"Women, who to prevent depravation of morals and ambiguity of issue, could not mix promiscuously in the public meetings of men."

"A lady who has been seen as a sloven or slut in the morning will never efface the impression she has made."

(To his daughter on her wedding day): *"The happiness of your life now depends on the continuing to please a single person. To this all other objects must be secondary, even your love for me."*

Jefferson was horrified by seeing women in public roles while visiting France, where liberalism had been birthed and then unleashed in a fury after the Revolution of 1789. He wrote to Washington that this meant that France was in a "desperate state" and that fortunately, for the happiness of men and women alike, this phenomenon did not "extend itself" to America as well.

Unfortunately, the words he wrote in the Declaration of Independence would later be twisted from their original meaning and used to justify that which he was staunchly against:

"All men are created equal."

Those five words, without a doubt, have been the most devastatingly consequential words in our entire history.

Both the suffragettes movement, which began in earnest in 1848 at the infamous Seneca Falls Convention and ended after winning women the right to vote in 1920, and the Negro "civil rights" movements borrowed heavily from Jefferson's Declaration – but the historical record speaks loud and clear on what his views on these matters actually were.

Idealistic liberals and outright enemies of America have blatantly twisted Jefferson's seemingly abstract words – as well as the words of other Founding Fathers – to push their own agendas.

This is not the Founders' fault, and given that these agendas run counter to American history and American interests, they are on their face an insult to these very men who are cited as their justification.

The 1848 Seneca Falls "Declaration of

Sentiments" quotes Jefferson virtually word for word, and then dishonestly applies it to women:

> We hold these truths to be self-evident: that all men and women are created equal; that they are endowed by their Creator with certain inalienable rights; that among these are life, liberty, and the pursuit of happiness; that to secure these rights governments are instituted, deriving their powers from the consent of the governed.

The above-stated views on women have only been overturned recently, really only since the second wave of feminism took off in the 60s.

For a while, those who still held these views were ridiculed for being "old-fashioned." Now that liberalism has so thoroughly taken hold, those of us who still hold these views – which, again, are the same as the Founding Fathers – are called "radicals." "Extremists," even.

What these views really are are normal. They are American. They are *white*.

The Founders were staunch proponents of Western (i.e. white) Civilization. All of their political ideas were formulated around what they thought was the best way to proceed with and advance Western Civilization while giving people as much freedom as possible and also keeping them morally upright and industrious.

As liberal policies based on "equality" are now clearly *destroying* Western Civilization, it stands to reason that the Founding Fathers would be on our side fighting against them, despite whatever abstract quotes can be cherry-picked from them to try and justify said civilization-wrecking policies.

They were not malicious people. They really did want freedom for all, to the best extent that that is possible.

What they certainly would've never stood for, though, is freedom for others, *at the expense of their own.*

With that in mind, we can safely say that any abstract ideas found among them – and there are some – about freeing blacks and then bringing them up to our level are now irrelevant, because the data is in and it shows that this is not possible and that even attempting to do so severely harms whites.

And for every one statement of an early American Founder pondering the possibility of peacefully integrating blacks that can be found – and these were just ideas, nothing close to freeing or integrating blacks en masse was ever practiced in their time – one could readily find a hundred saying that this would never work and that they must be removed.

We can debate over which aspects of America's founding ideology were flawed, and some of it without a doubt was, but what is not debatable is that America was set up for the 'posterity' of the Founders and the white founding stock that settled, conquered and built it.

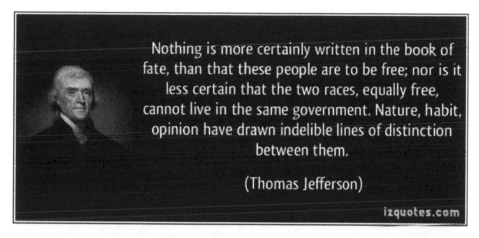

Nothing is more certainly written in the book of fate, than that these people are to be free; nor is it less certain that the two races, equally free, cannot live in the same government. Nature, habit, opinion have drawn indelible lines of distinction between them.

(Thomas Jefferson)

izquotes.com

Race was the binding force of early America. One of the first acts of Congress, the Naturalization Act of 1790, restricted immigration and citizenship to "free white persons of good character."

By fighting to protect the well-being of the white stock of America, we on the Alt-Right are merely carrying on what the Founders tilled, toiled, fought and bled for – while those who are not with us are complicit in throwing it all away.

The amount of broken homes of white families of the innocent victims who have been raped, murdered and maimed by black and other non-white criminals among us is absolutely heartwrenching once you become aware of the statistics, which are actively covered up by our alien-occupied media and academia.

The Alt-Right is aware of these ugly racial realities, and we just want to put an end to them, yet for this we are called evil "haters."

We're not allowed to say these things in polite society because it might hurt the feelings of non-whites.

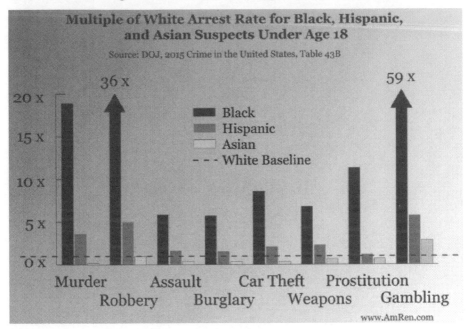

That is the reality of the feminized, liberalized and Judaized system and society we now find ourselves living under.

It wants us silenced. It wants us dead, even, simply because we tell the truth.

But we're not going to be silent, and we're not going to back down because we know that what we are doing is right.

Innocent whites raped and murdered by non-whites by the tens of thousands annually is what is *truly evil* to us, and no amount of epithets is ever going to intimidate us into denying that.

We know for a fact now that blacks are incapable of functioning in civilization. They are only capable of destroying it. Therefore we want them *out*. We want to send them back, regardless if it hurts their feelings.

That is the mature, adult way to handle this.

That's how the hard men who initially built this nation would've handled it.

Just go ask the Indians – if you can find any.

Our government is now anti-white, meaning it is un-American. We, the people, therefore have the right and the duty to fight to take it back so it will again serve our interests, as it was originally intended.

This anti-white/unAmerican nature of our society is more transparent now than ever. Black sportsball players who get paid millions of dollars to

15

throw a ball around are purposefully disrespecting our National Anthem – and they're being celebrated in the media for it. Meanwhile, those of us who have been trying to protect the toppling of our historical statues and monuments, in Charlottesville and elsewhere, are being aggressively demonized and persecuted from all angles.

And while the Alt-Right is being censored and shut down at an alarming rate, the so-called "right-wing" in America is doing virtually nothing to support us, and in many cases is even joining the ranks of our enemies in opposition to us.

At least the liberals, Jews, blacks and other anti-whites who are actively tearing down our statues and monuments and disrespecting the National Anthem and American Flag instinctively, if not consciously, realize that an attack on America is an attack on white people in general.

That's why they're attacking America in the first place.

It's a racial attack against *us*.

The so-called "conservatives" – *cuckservatives* – who want to bury their head in the sand and run away from the race question are some of the worst, most pathetic, sniveling cowards ever to walk the face of the earth.

They are a disgrace to the Founding Fathers that they claim to revere. They have conserved nothing and instead have already lost just about everything that this nation once held dear, and in their cowardice they will only continue losing until even their own genetic legacy is wiped off the map and then scrubbed from the history books.

Jesse Benn, Contributor
Dad, partner, engaged citizen, opinionated writer, leftist, PhD student.

White Athletes Still Standing For The Anthem Are Standing For White Supremacy

It's a question of privilege.

09/25/2017 04:08 am ET | **Updated** 1 day ago

They are #FakePatriots, and they need to be bullied – mercilessly – until they either join our side or get the hell out of our way.

The main reason these modern-day "conservatives," patriotards, and the like either take the view that our Founding Fathers weren't actually racist, or that their racism was just an unfortunate part of our history that thankfully we have now moved past, is because they have been gaslit by the media into thinking being "racist" is the worst thing one could possibly be.

"Racism" has become the absolute moral standard for evil.

This has not been accomplished by logic and

debate, but by emotional manipulation and abuse.

The media constantly shows images and sends messages that are meant to induce whites into feeling guilty.

Patriotism Is for White People

 Terrell Jermaine Starr
Monday 12:39pm

Filed to: PATRIOTISM ⌄

🔥 112.7K   💬 199   ☆ 49   ⋮

If we controlled the media we could just as easily use pictures of victims of non-white crime and swing people in the exact opposite direction.

In fact, it would be much easier to condition people toward our way of thinking rather than the current way, since racism is the natural and healthy, default position of humans.

What if the case of Mona Nelson – which barely made the news – was broadcast nonstop instead of George Zimmerman and Trayvon Martin? Ever heard of Mona Nelson? She kidnapped and tortured a 12-year-old white child to death with a welding torch and then dumped his body in a ditch – on Christmas Eve! His body was so badly burned it had to be identified by dental records.

Convincing people to go against their own nature requires almost nonstop brainwashing on all fronts, day after day, from cradle to grave – which is what we've had in America since the Jews have taken control. Certainly since before I was born; probably before my parents were.

I sympathize with my white brothers, who have all undergone this intense brainwashing, and I understand that playing on guilt feelings is a powerful weakness of whites that has been exploited by our enemies to the fullest – but it's time to grow some balls. The clock is ticking. We don't have time to pussyfoot around anymore.

Come over to reality and just admit that America was never intended to be a "proposition nation," a "melting pot," or any other such gibberish.

It was never intended to be a multicultural experiment. That crazy idea came much later and is a blatant perversion of what this country was originally envisioned as, and a slap in the face to the great white men who built it.

Even if the multicultural experiment was created in good faith: at what point do we admit that the experiment is a failure?

We won't admit it though because now it has become a moral imperative. We are expected to hand over our country to foreigners. Those of us who object to this idea are now unironically referred to as "nazi terrorists." That's how far we've fallen: "nazi terrorist" is now a legitimate euphemism for "those who don't want to be replaced by people who hate them in the country that their ancestors built."

Part of the stated justification for this moral imperative is payback for slavery. Well, the Founding

Fathers did not invent slavery – they inherited it. And most of them were against it.

The "melting pot" idea comes from a play written by the Jew Israel Zangwill in 1908 – well over 100 years after Our Nation's founding.

Lincoln, Jefferson, Franklin and Washington were all White Separatists – White Nationalists.

That is what we who fall under the moniker of "Alt-Right" are as well.

There are inevitably many small differences between us and them, of course, as technology has drastically changed the world since their time and we now have the hindsight to see what worked and what didn't – but the core tenets remain exactly the same.

> I will say then that I am not, nor ever have been in favor of bringing about in anyway the social and political equality of the white and black races.

Abraham Lincoln

If they could see this mess we're in today, I've no doubt they would go back and put measures in place to prevent it all as best they could. They would draft legislation designed to safeguard us – their posterity – from all of this degeneracy, from the dysgenics, from the Jews taking over and from the hordes of non-whites spilling across our borders.

But, of course, they were merely men and not prophets.

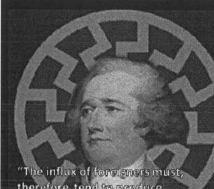

"The influx of foreigners must, therefore, tend to produce a heterogeneous compound; to change and corrupt the national spirit; to complicate and confound public opinion; to introduce foreign propensities."

HAMILTON

"To be consistent with existing and probably unalterable prejudices in the U.S. freed blacks ought to be permanently removed beyond the region occupied by or allotted to a White population."

MADISON

"[T]he Number of purely white People in the World is proportionably very small.... I could wish their Numbers were increased.... But perhaps I am partial to the Complexion of my Country, for such Kind of Partiality is natural to Mankind."

FRANKLIN

"Providence has been pleased to give this one connected country to one united people--a people descended from the same ancestors, speaking the same language, professing the same religion, attached to the same principles of government, very similar in their manners and customs."

JAY

23

They did the best they could.

Now it's up to us, the only ones who are still truly fighting for the Founders true vision of America, to fix this mess – or die trying.

Anything less and we wouldn't even be worthy of the title "American." At this point, unfortunately – most aren't.

Hopefully, one day soon, they will join us though.

We are the only option left.

These are the undeniable facts:

The Alt-Right is White Nationalism.

White Nationalism is Americanism.

Deal with it.

Originally published on October 1, 2017

White Racialism and American Nationalism Pt. 1

There has been a sustained, nonstop assault on DS ever since we suggested the Alt-Right should present itself more explicitly as American Nationalist – as the only movement who has the true interests of white Americans at heart – by those who are opposed to such a stance.

Everything has seemingly fallen into place for this to be the next logical step: We became famous for a rally that, despite its setbacks, showed us to be the only ones with the courage to stand up against the toppling of our national monuments. At the same time the country has become, and continues to become, increasingly racially polarized.

Black football players take a knee to spite our

National Anthem, our President is called a "Nazi" and a "racist" constantly and the Jews and their allies are now overtly attacking America as an inherently white supremacist nation.

MJ Rosenberg, Contributor
Worked on Capitol Hill for Democratic Senators and House members for 20 years

Trump Gets It: Racism Is As American As Apple Pie

09/28/2017 11:58 am ET | **Updated** 7 hours ago

The fact that even after 6 months we have been crippled in this strategy not by the left, but by those who are ostensibly on our side, has been quite a shocking thing to behold, to say the least.

If anything, it has brought to the surface the inherent folly of a "big tent" strategy, which may ultimately be a positive in the long term, despite the inescapable growing pains. Better for the fallout to come now rather than later, I suppose.

Many (but not all) critics of the American Nationalist stance seem to think that presenting ourselves as anything less than unironic, hardcore National Socialists is somehow a form of cucking.

It's true, of course, that ever since WWII any time a white person has advocated for their own interests they have been roundly smeared as a "Nazi," and that this has been a frighteningly effective way of silencing any and all opposition to the anti-white system.

For this reason, it was necessary to neutralize this tactic of our enemies. The Alt-Right accomplished this, brilliantly, through the use of ironic and semi-ironic Nazism, trolling, and refusing to go on the defensive.

Thanks to the far-reaching and tireless spreading of edgy, educational memes and Alt-Right internet culture in general – which Daily Stormer has played, and will continue to play, a large role in – young white males have been thoroughly desensitized to the stigma attached to the "Nazi" label.

Now that this taboo is broken, and we have forced the world to take notice of us and the "Alt-Right" is a household name, it just makes sense to change tack in order to broaden our outreach – to move into a more serious, but still fun, "phase two," if you will.

This is quite similar to what the founder of white nationalism himself, George Lincoln Rockwell, had been doing in his time. He used Nazi imagery and shock tactics to make himself irresistible to the media, who otherwise just ignored him. This made him a household name, but was only "phase one" of a clearly laid out four phase plan (which in hindsight was not without its flaws, to be sure).

Shortly before he was assassinated, he moved into "phase two." This entailed dropping the Nazi uniform, changing the name of his party from the American Nazi Party to the National Socialist's White People's Party and using the fame and attention he had acquired to educate the public on the plight of the white race in America.

Dr. William Pierce, who was the editor of Rockwell's journal, only formally joined the party after the name change. Following Rockwell's untimely death, Pierce still wanted to move forward with the more serious "phase two" strategy, but the movement instead rapidly reverted back to the "Hollywood Nazi" type approach, causing him to split.

He later said of Matt Koehl, who ended up being Rockwell's successor:

> Koehl was an admirable guy in some ways. For one thing, he was very reliable–but he wasn't very imaginative. To figure out what to do he would take out Mein Kampf or see how Hitler did it in 1928. I said, 'Jesus, Matt, we've

got a different situation now.'

After the split, and shortly before the official founding of the "National Alliance" – by far the most successful American white nationalist organization in history – Pierce wrote the essay "Prospectus for a National Front" (1970), in which he advocated for a more American-tailored approach and advised against "isolating ourselves from the public with programs and images so radical that only a small fraction of one percent will respond."

He said to his biographer, Robert Griffin, about this change in direction:

> I was certain there were many people around who didn't think of themselves as National Socialists who were concerned about the same degenerative trends in politics and demographics as I was, and I wanted to find them.

That many white racialists become enamored with National Socialism is quite understandable. We all get redpilled on the state of the world, we see the Jews ruling over us and how our race is being destroyed, and then it dawns on us that Hitler was openly fighting against it.

What this has resulted in is a thread of thought in the Alt-Right, and the White Nationalist community in general, that Germany was the one country to stand up to the Jews, and that the rest of our people and nations were completely enslaved to them, even back then.

This is a very simplified, and in my view poisonous, view of an extremely complex history. First off, it must be kept in mind that what brought the Nazis to power was a unique set of historical circumstances that just weren't present in America or elsewhere.

By 1967 Rockwell had dropped the Nazi outfit and was wearing a suit.

Germany had been defeated in WWI and were humiliated and crushed by the Versailles Treaty, genocidal, Godless communism was at their doorstep and Jewish power and subversion was much further advanced and entrenched there than anywhere else.

America back then was still a traditional, wholesome white society. Degeneracy was outlawed pretty much across the board, Jews were looked down upon and blacks, who were our primary racial problem, were more or less kept in check.

31

So, while our ideology does indeed parallel that of the Nazis in many ways, it isn't necessarily more German or National Socialist than it is American.

Hitler had many great ideas – but not many of them were particularly original. Race and eugenics, for instance, were mainstream, accepted science at that time.

Of the most influential early racial thinkers, really only one was a German: Ernst Haeckel.

The rest were French (de Gobineau), British (Chamberlain, Galton, Darwin) and, most of all, American (Grant, Ripley, Davenport, Stoddard, Goddard, Walker).

Hitler, and the Nazis in general, were heavily influenced by certain American personalities and American racial laws.

Alfred Rosenberg, in his *The Myth of the 20th Century* – probably the second most influential ideological book of the Third Reich, next to *Mein Kampf* – wrote this:

> The United states of America, according to the universal agreement of all travellers, is the magnificent land of the future. It has the great task of throwing aside all outworn ideas which date from before its foundation. It can proceed with youthful strength to set up the new idea of the racial state, such as some awakened Americans have already apprehended, like Grant and Stoddard.

They saw the necessity for the expulsion and resettlement of the Blacks and the Yellow men, the handing over of east Asiatic possessions to Japan, the working toward a Black colonisation in central Africa, and the resettlement of the Jews to a region where this entire group can find a place.

The Nazi writer Albrecht Wirth, in a 1934 book designed to teach Germans global history through a racial lens, *Völkisch World History*, wrote the following:

> The most important event in the history of the states of the Second Millennium—up until the [First World] War—was the founding of the United States of America. The struggle of the Aryans for world domination received thereby its strongest prop.

A second book of the same nature, *The Supremacy of the White Race*, written by Wahrhold Drascher in 1936 called America "the [leader] of the white peoples" and said its Founding was "the first fateful turning point" in the struggle for global White Supremacy. "[A] conscious unity of the white race" would have never emerged without it, Drascher contended.

Comments such as these among the Nazis are countless. Hitler himself, though very critical of America at times as well, had much praise for and drew much inspiration from America in regard to his racial views and policies. He writes explicitly of the 1924 Immigration Act in *Mein Kampf*:

At present there exists one State which manifests at least some modest attempts that show a better appreciation of how things ought to be done in this matter. It is not, however, in our model German Republic but in the U.S.A. that efforts are made to conform at least partly to the counsels of commonsense. By refusing immigrants to enter there if they are in a bad state of health, and by excluding certain races from the right to become naturalized as citizens, they have begun to introduce principles similar to those on which we wish to ground the People's State.

In his unpublished second book, Hitler commended America for rejecting the Jewish "Melting Pot" idea and shifting immigration policy so that the majority taken in were Northern Europeans, the original founding stock.

The 1924 Immigration Act, also known as the "National Origins Act" or the "Johnson-Reed Act," was explicitly pro-white – and implicitly anti-Jewish – legislation. It passed in the House by a vote of 308 to 62, and in the Senate 69 to 9.

During the run up to the passing of the bill, Madison Grant, who was the main driving force behind it and the most influential racial author of the time, said to then sitting President, Howard Taft:

vast floods of utterly alien races and types are

pouring in, and the great cities are being swamped by the Polish Jews from Eastern Europe. Anyone who scientifically faces the facts can understand the extremely inferior and immoral structure of these latter, and it is universally admitted and deplored in private conversation.

Grant said that the influx of Eastern European Jews was "by far the most serious immigration matter that now confronts us" and that the Act was "the only chance of our life time to shut out the Jews. It is now or never."

US foreign service officials, according to Jonathan Spiro's biography of Grant, warned that the Jews were "filthy and ignorant and the majority are verminous"; that they were "abnormally twisted, . . . un-American, and often dangerous in their habits"; and that they were a "thoroughly undesirable" class of immigrant and unquestionably "unassimilable."[*]

Burton J. Hendrick publicly admitted in 1923 that the Emergency Quota Act of 1921 was "chiefly intended—it is just as well to be frank about the matter—to restrict the entrance of Jews from eastern Europe."

Albert Johnson, one of two main architects of the Act, brought State Department cables before the Senate Immigration Committee which warned that the Jews preparing to sail to America were "evasive, dishonest, and . . . do not have the moral qualifications for American citizenship."

Spiro continues:

Johnson read aloud to the House fresh consular cables provided by the State Department, warning that the majority of

---

[*] Jonathan Spiro, *Defending the Master Race: Conservation, Eugenics, and the Legacy of Madison Grant*, 2008, p. 206

European Jews embarking for the United States were "subnormal," "twisted," "deteriorated," and full of "perverted ideas. . . . These are not those who hewed the forests, . . . conquered the wastes, and built America. These are beaten folk" who, "besides being as a class economic parasites, . . . are impregnated with Bolshevism."

In short, according to the U.S. State Department, "this type of immigrant is not desirable from any point of view at this time."

The 1924 Immigration quotas held even as Jews were being increasingly persecuted under Hitler. In 1939, even following Kristallnacht, only 8% of Americans polled said they wanted to accept more Jewish refugees. That same year, the final attempt to increase the quota – the Wagner-Rogers bill, which called for refuge for Jewish children specifically – was soundly defeated.

"One year later," writes Spiro, "a similar bill to admit British children was introduced into the U.S. Congress. It was quickly approved."

In fact, no Western nation would accept an increase in Jews. In 1938, representatives from 32 countries organized the Évian Conference to decide what to do about the ones then living under Nazi rule.

The one Jewish representative who was invited to the conference, Golda Meir, wasn't even allowed to speak. The only two countries in attendance that were willing to take in Jewish refugees were non-white – the Dominican Republic and Costa Rica.

Jews who were liberated from concentration camps following the war, far from being given refuge en masse, were instead put into displaced persons camps, where they had to stay for indefinite periods of time until they could be repatriated to their countries of origin. As many Jews feared persecution in those countries, they were forced to continue their underground network to Palestine (which was illegal at the time, as the British had barred their further immigration).

This shows us that, aside from a few treacherous elites such as FDR, Americans (and other Europeans) had no special love for the Jews. Most Americans, having little to no contact with Jews, were probably indifferent to them at best.

Blacks, who whites had much more experience with, were at the time of WWII still almost universally seen as inferior and as a mortal danger to whites.[*]

were probably accurate. While a 1944 poll suggested that 12 percent of non-Jews "appear to be definitely anti-Semitic" and 42 percent "suscepti-ble" to anti-Semitic propaganda, a 1943 poll revealed that "90 percent of the American people stated that they would rather loose [sic] the war than give full equality to the American Negroes."[19]

There was no official legislation targeting the Jews by name in America, but they were effectively shut out of higher institutions by quotas and other

---

[*] Cheryl Lynn Greenberg, *Troubling the Waters: Black-Jewish Relations in the American Century*, 2010, p. 81

regulations specifically designed to limit their numbers, just as the Immigration Act was.

For example, the dean of Harvard law school, Roscoe Pound (1916-1936), who is one of the most cited legal scholars in American history, was an open admirer of Hitler, saying he "was a man who can bring [Austria and Germany] freedom from agitating `movements.'"

Lawrence Lowell, who was president of Harvard until 1933, also admired the Nazis – sending representatives to Nazi Universities even as their ongoing persecution of the Jews was well-known – and worked feverishly to limit Jewish and black enrollment at Harvard. He also led the Secret Court of 1920, which purged the institution of homosexuals.

The most popular radio personality during the 30s was Father Charles Coughlin, whose broadcasts were openly anti-Semitic. At its peak his show had a listenership of up to 40 million (out of a population of roughly 120-130 million).

Hitler's private train, which took him to his "Eagle's Nest" retreat, was code named Amerika, because he so much admired US industrial strength and transportation ability.[*]

He especially admired the great American industrialist Henry Ford, who was also a highly vocal and influential anti-Semite. Hitler praised Ford by name in *Mein Kampf*, had a life sized portrait of him

---

[*] Klaus P. Fischer, *Hitler and America*, 2011, p. 9

next to his desk, and modeled the Volkswagon on the Model T.

Father Charles Coughlin

"You can tell Herr Ford that I am a great admirer of his," Hitler told Prince Louis Ferdinand as he departed for the United States. "I shall do my best to put his theories into practice in Germany."

In 1937, on Ford's 75th birthday, Hitler awarded him the Grand Cross of the German Eagle – the highest honor that could be given to a foreigner.

Ford spent millions of his own money to wake the world to the Jewish menace, printing a total of 91 anti-Semitic articles in his *Dearborn Independent*, which he gave out free to every customer.

Henry Ford receiving the Grand Cross

Even Baldur Von Schirach, head of the Hitler Youth, was redpilled on the JQ by the *Dearborn Independent* articles when he was 17.

They influenced Hitler's view on the Jews as well, and are quoted in *Mein Kampf*. Theodor Fritsch, Germany's leading anti-Jewish publisher, translated and distributed them widely in Germany.

A core tenet of Hitler's ideology was German expansionism: lebensraum. He was openly inspired in this endeavor by the conquest of America – "Manifest Destiny" - and the British Empire. He considered Americans as well as the British as cousins to the Germans, as being cut from the same superior racial stock, and thus deserving of world mastery.

Germany, in his eyes, belonged at the apex alongside these two Nordic superpowers, as it was prior to WWI. He was playing catch up, not blazing any trails.

Dr. Adrienne Keene ✔ @NativeApprops · Aug 15, 2017

Why the Nazis Loved America time.com/4703586/nazis-... (From March)

Why the Nazis Loved America
The terrible history of racist laws
time.com

Dr. Adrienne Keene ✔
@NativeApprops

"In 1928, Hitler praised the Americans for having 'gunned down the millions of Redskins to a few hundred thousand'"

♡ 230   8:11 PM - Aug 15, 2017

💬 260 people are talking about this   ›

The infamous 1934 "Nuremberg Laws" were heavily influenced by – and wouldn't have come into existence without – America's "anti-miscegenation" laws, which banned marriage between a white and a non-white in 30 states.

Virginia – the land of Jefferson – was home to the infamous Racial Integrity Act of 1924. This Act designated people as non-white by the "one-drop rule," This was significantly more hardcore than the Nuremberg Laws – "too racist" for the Nazis to copy.

These laws were lobbied for, and inspired by, the fiercely patriotic Madison Grant, whose lifetime achievements are absolutely breathtaking. He counted multiple U.S. Presidents as his friends including fellow white racialist Teddy Roosevelt (1901-1909) and Herbert Hoover (1929-1933).

Aside from popularizing race science and getting an impressive amount of pro-white legislation passed, Grant also led the way in creating the conservationist movement. The American bison, and dozens of other animals, would be extinct today if it weren't for Grant.

In 1899, he founded the Bronx Zoo, which was four times larger than any other existing Zoo in the world and the first to attempt to recreate the animals' natural habitats.

An African Pygmy, Ota Benga, was displayed in the Zoo as a semi-human evolutionary curiosity.

Now I have to ask: How does using an African as a zoo exhibit jive with the assertion, made by many who are ostensibly on our side, that America was destined to be cucked or is the inevitable outcome of the phrase "all men are created equal"?

It doesn't. Our biggest problem – our true fatal mistake – according to the bulk of the Alt-Right, has not been a handful of later-misinterpreted Enlightenment-inspired platitudes, but that we allowed Jews in our midst and then failed to deal with them properly.

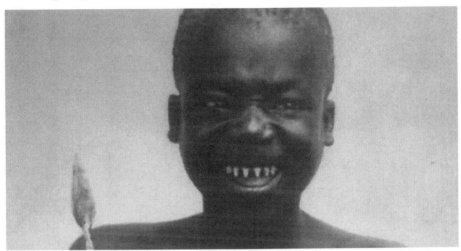

Ota Benga

After giving much thought as to why the above described period of our history is generally blacked out or glossed over, even while liberals love to beat us over the head with our "racist legacy," I've concluded that it is because America has become such an engine of progressivism they prefer it to seem as though our history has been an uninterrupted, if slow-going, move toward egalitarianism, and these facts shatter that myth.

Therefore, those on the right who cherry pick

quotes by the Founding Fathers to craft a narrative of American history being essentially a straight line to the left, from the signing of the Declaration of Independence to today, are in that regard undeniably marching in lockstep with the anti-American liberal left.

These points will be addressed further in part 2 of this article.

Originally published on March 25, 2018

White Racialism and American Nationalism Pt. 2

Some of the people who countersignal the concept of American Nationalism do so because they have an agenda that is entirely different than the majority of what we call the "Alt-Right."

They either belong to a foreign religion that Americans have never subscribed to in significant numbers, are Southern Nationalists who want to bring back the Confederacy and think Yankees are worse than Jews, will accept nothing less than overt National Socialism, or are only interested in terrorism and violent revolution.

Therefore, it's becoming clear that it is futile to try and find common ground with these people. They are not, and will probably never be, on the same page as us, and it's a shame they have caused a debate over whether or not we should consider ourselves American Nationalists to go on for this long.

While most of these people are indeed "pro-white," that alone is not sufficient to justify a formal alliance when the extent of our differences are considered (though we can certainly have mutual respect with some while doing our own things). At best we will just repeatedly butt heads, at worst they will use our popularity and what we have built for their own personal gain.

This land is ours.

Others, I assume, are none of the above, but have been gaslit by those who are. It is for this reason I will address some of the more common arguments put forth against American Nationalism, and further show why I think being anti-American is antithetical to common sense and counterproductive to what we are trying to accomplish.

The more sophisticated of these arguments involves the formulation of a narrative that paints America as having had a Civic Nationalist foundation from its very inception. They claim that America was based on Enlightenment principles that essentially sealed its fate as a multiracial state.

I will not spend much time refuting this, as it seems to come mainly from Southern Nationalists who hate Yankees and are still mad about the Civil War and the destructive racial policies that were imposed on them by the North.

It goes without saying, for those of us without a historical grudge against our own people, that critiquing our Founding Fathers (who were, clearly and demonstrably, white nationalists and traditionalists) as crazy liberals who laid the foundation for the later destruction of their own nation and people is a transparently self-defeating strategy.

When one considers the source, it's hard for one to believe that this view was arrived at through honest intellectual inquiry rather than a desire to deliberately undercut American identity at its roots, similar to the "critical theory" of the anti-American left that seeks to "deconstruct whiteness."

The same technique could be used to form a

similar narrative against the South (who wanted to import even *more* blacks prior to the Civil War), or any other white country or area, if one were so inclined, just as it could be used to blame Christianity, rather than the Enlightenment, for our racial decline.

We are not doing that, though, because we consider Southerners, Christians and all whites worldwide as our brothers and see no benefit in tearing down the very people we are trying to save.

Demonizing our history and delegitimizing us as a people is a tactic the left uses to blackpill us into submission – to get us to accept our own displacement. This kind of negativity has no place in a pro-white movement.

We are trying to uplift our people and build better men and give them something to fight for, not fill them with despair.

Though there is much for us to learn from

Fascism and National Socialism, the American system wasn't always the shitshow that it is today. Originally, voting was restricted to educated, land-owning white males over the age of 21 – those who had a direct "stake in society."

Only about 1.8% of the population are estimated to have voted in the first Presidential election (unanimously for Washington), with a maximum of 6% being eligible at that time. Jews were excluded.

Even Oswald Mosley – one of our greatest thinkers – wrote that his British Union of Fascists were only against the "perversion of democracy" and that

> democracy in its true sense — government of the people, by the people, for the people, as an expression of the natural, healthy will of the people when free from the deception of financial politics — was exactly what we wanted.

The Founding Fathers were only egalitarians in the sense of equality under the law and equality of opportunity, based on the Enlightenment concept of meritocracy. As Mosley explains:

> Equality of opportunity is a fundamental thing. Let those rule who are fitted to rule. Let no man rule because his grandfather proved himself fitted to rule. [The Enlightenment] was a revolt against privilege, an affirmation that the man of talent and of capacity should be the man to conduct the affairs of a great

50

nation.[*]

It was only later that "all men are created equal" was deliberately misinterpreted to mean men are equal in ability, or that the races are equal. In the Founding Fathers' time, blacks weren't even considered human, much less "equal." That idea is patently absurd.

The American system as it was originally intended is not at all incompatible with fascism. In fact, there are fasces all over the place in America. They symbolize the Roman concept of "strength through unity," thus stand as a living testament that the Jewish idea that "diversity is our strength" is what is truly incompatible with Americanism.

Fasces were still being incorporated into architecture well into the 20s and 30s, as many Americans at that time openly admired Mussolini and what he had done for the Italian people.

In contrast to the confusing, esoteric gibberish about the Enlightenment that these anti-American racialists push, the Alt-Right generally has a much simpler message: we have a Jewish problem.

That doesn't mean that we deny having problems of our own, or that Jewish subversion didn't require already existing flaws in our society. It means that we recognize that a distinct racial enemy has infiltrated every level of our society and has demonstrably – in many cases admittedly – remolded

---

* Oswald Mosley, *My Life*, 1968, p. 270

SIR OSWALD MOSLEY

it and reinterpreted our history to suit his own ends.

Even if Jews aren't the original sickness that is killing our race (maybe that is our individualist nature – who knows), no honest person can deny that they have accelerated it to a frightening degree, and are the ones found blocking the way toward any solution.

Fasces in America.

There is not a racial disaster in this country since the Civil War in which you don't see the Jews front and center.

It was Jews who led the Civil Rights movement. It was Jews who invented the concept that "race is a social construct" (Franz Boas et. al.). It was a Jew who invented the idea of America as a "Melting Pot" (Israel Zangwill) and it was a Jew who invented the concept of "cultural pluralism" i.e. "multiculturalism" (Horace Kallen).

Jews founded and run the ADL, and they dominate the SPLC and the ACLU.

The Jews have pushed, and continue to push, nonstop anti-white vitriol using their vast propaganda network which includes major publishing houses, academia, the mainstream media and the entirety of Hollywood.

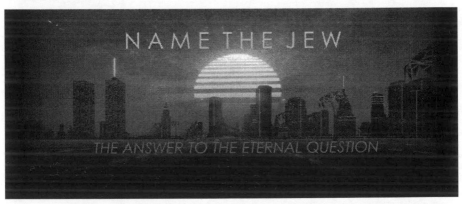

With their hypersensitive racial consciousness they hunt down and enforce political correctness on anyone who even mildly questions them, keeping the populace in a constant state of fear as everyone knows – whether consciously or unconsciously – that if they step out of the bounds of the anti-white, Jewish narrative their reputation and career will be swiftly and ruthlessly destroyed.

This pernicious influence is the number one problem facing our people today, and working to free

Join today!

them from it – rather than merely blaming ourselves for our current predicament – is an act of fierce patriotism and nationalism; an act of love for our race that is perfectly in keeping with the spirit of our Founding Fathers who hated and fought against lies and tyranny with every fiber of their being.

America was by no means "destined" to become what it has become. In fact, there's every reason to believe that we were well on our way to correcting the racial blunder of the Civil War, had the Jews not repeatedly thrown a stick in our spokes.

The science of race didn't really come into focus until the latter half of the 19th century, following the theories of Darwin and de Gobineau (which Southern intellectuals, by the way, simply used to make absurd justifications for slavery). Like many of the mistakes of the Founding Fathers, it was an "unknown," therefore hardly something that can be held against them.

Following the Civil War (for which there is plenty of blame to go around on both sides), Northerners and Southerners alike allied in support of the American Colonization Society, which had been created in 1816 and was initially supported by leading American Founders such as Thomas Jefferson, Andrew Jackson and James Madison, and which had as its mission sending American blacks back to Africa.

After the release of Madison Grant's book *The Passing of the Great Race* in 1916, scientific racism became the dominant view among the American elite.

Theodore Roosevelt wrote of it in Scribner's magazine:

> The book is a capital book; in purpose, in vision, in grasp of the facts our people most need to realize. It shows an extraordinary range of reading and a wide scholarship. It shows a habit of singular serious thought on the subject of most commanding importance. It shows a fine fearlessness in assailing the popular and mischievous sentimentalities and attractive and corroding falsehoods which few men dare assail. It is the work of an American scholar and gentleman; and all Americans should be sincerely grateful to you for writing it.

Its influence reached much further than just America, though. Hitler, for instance, called the book his "Bible." The seminal chapter in *Mein Kampf*, "Race and People," which so much informed Nazi policy, was essentially just a summary of the Grantian worldview.

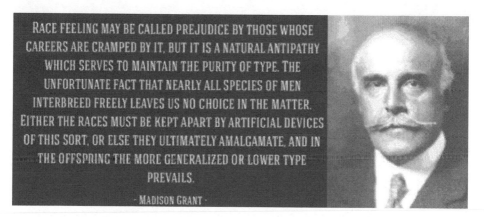

RACE FEELING MAY BE CALLED PREJUDICE BY THOSE WHOSE CAREERS ARE CRAMPED BY IT, BUT IT IS A NATURAL ANTIPATHY WHICH SERVES TO MAINTAIN THE PURITY OF TYPE. THE UNFORTUNATE FACT THAT NEARLY ALL SPECIES OF MEN INTERBREED FREELY LEAVES US NO CHOICE IN THE MATTER. EITHER THE RACES MUST BE KEPT APART BY ARTIFICIAL DEVICES OF THIS SORT, OR ELSE THEY ULTIMATELY AMALGAMATE, AND IN THE OFFSPRING THE MORE GENERALIZED OR LOWER TYPE PREVAILS.

- MADISON GRANT -

Around this same time, a black nationalist named Marcus Garvey was making significant headway in America. Garvey, who admired the nationalistic passion of both Hitler and Mussolini, wanted to instill racial pride in his people by leading them toward self-determination. His organization, the Universal Negro Improvement Association (UNIA), founded in 1917, boasted 2 million members by 1919, and as many as 6 million by 1926 (when the black population of the United States was no more than 11.5 million).

Madison Grant, whose main mission in life was to secure the existence of the white race, naturally wanted the blacks shipped back to Africa as well, so he formed a strong alliance with Garvey following a back-to-Africa speech Garvey made in Madison Square Garden in 1920.

Garvey originally modeled himself on the founder of Zionism, Theodor Herzl, and was sympathetic to Jews early in his career, but he grew increasingly anti-Semitic as he saw the Jews thwarting his mission at every turn.

The radical Jewish-led NAACP, which with their mulatto figurehead W.E.B. DuBois promoted integration over separation, dedicated much of their energy to destroying Garvey (just as Jews would later promote communist integrationist Martin Luther King Jr. over popular black nationalist Malcolm X).

When Garvey had visited NAACP headquarters

in 1917, he famously "stormed out" muttering about it being a "white [which he would later realize actually meant "Jewish"] organization."

Garvey was, unfortunately, eventually destroyed – and his movement rendered stillborn – after being tried and convicted for mail fraud.

The Judge who convicted him, Julian Mack, was the former head of the American Jewish Congress and the Zionist Organization of America. "When they wanted to get me," Garvey complained, "they had a Jewish judge try me, and a Jewish prosecutor. I would have been freed but two Jews on the jury held out against me ten hours and succeeded in convicting me, whereupon the Jewish judge gave me the maximum penalty."

Garvey's meteoric rise is clear evidence that racial self-determination is the natural and desirable state for all peoples, and his downfall shows yet another example of the Jews' historically being the primary agitators against such an arrangement, even while they hypocritically support their own racially exclusive State of Israel.

Elite American racialists, led by Grant, also desired to deport the Jews, but saw that as a much more difficult task than deporting blacks, given the power that the Jews had already accumulated.

Eugenicist Charles Davenport, in a letter to Grant in 1925, suggested jokingly that he thought maybe it would be best to just incinerate the Jews as the Puritans did the witches, but unfortunately it was "against the mores to burn any considerable part of our population."

Grant's main nemesis was the Jewish immigrant Franz Boas, who was driven by the fear that race science would lead to increasing levels of anti-Semitism. This fear was not unfounded.

In *The Passing of the Great Race*, Grant wrote that the Polish Jew's "dwarf stature, peculiar mentality and ruthless concentration on self-interest" was being "engrafted upon the stock of the nation," and warned of the consequences of race-mixing as follows:

> Whether we like to admit it or not, the result
> of the mixture of two races, in the long run,
> gives us a race reverting to the more ancient,

generalized and lower type. The cross between a white man and an Indian is an Indian; the cross between a white man and a Negro is a Negro; the cross between a white man and a Hindu is a Hindu; and the cross between any of the three European races and a Jew is a Jew.

Charles Davenport: Total Shitlord.

This passage was quoted or paraphrased in hundreds of other anthropological and scientific works following the release of *The Passing of the Great Race*, and eventually helped lead to the "shutting out" of the Jews with the Immigration Act of 1924.

Boas, though, was a very committed and

formidable foe, and world historical events would eventually turn things in his favor in a big way – as we'll see in the third and final part of this article.

Originally published on April 2, 2018

White Racialism and American Nationalism Pt. 3

When we are accused of blaming the Jews for our woes our response is: yes, we blame the Jews. That doesn't mean we deny having problems of our own or consider whites blameless, it means we recognize the issues that are leading to the irreversible destruction of our race and nation as stemming almost exclusively from Jewish intellectuals and Jewish activists.

This is not something that is up for debate.

Those on the front line preventing whites from coming to any rational solutions to our problems are overwhelmingly Jewish, as well. Even when whites may indirectly benefit, such as in the case of policies proposed by Donald Trump, we see a full court press by Jews trying to destroy him politically and condemning him in the harshest and most hysterical terms imaginable on every organ of their far-reaching and virtually all-encompassing media.

If it weren't for one charismatic and unscrupulous Jewish "scientist" in the early 20th century, Franz Boas, Darwinian racial science would've won the day in America, by default. Boas put a scientific veneer on what before was only an abstract liberal delusion: the idea that all races are "equal."

Franz Boas

The two main schools of anthropological thought at that time were those of Boas and of Madison Grant. This was in essence a struggle between whites and Jews – between European-driven science (biological anthropology) and Jewish ethnic activist-based pseudoscience ("cultural anthropology").

America, being as large as it is, was never monolithic on the topic of race. In the theoretical realm there had been high-minded ideas about racial equality stretching back to its earliest days, stemming generally from Enlightenment philosophy ("nurture over nature") and some of the more radical Christian sects such as the Quakers ("all are equal in the eyes of God"). Nevertheless, white supremacy and inequality were assumed by the vast majority (about 90%) of the population prior to the 1950s.

While Grant condensed decades worth of racial theory and science into his work, Boas had almost no predecessors. He was a far-left, anti-racist activist who faked data to bolster his political agenda. Over two thirds of his most important disciples were Jews, and over time they pushed out of anthropology everybody that didn't toe the Boasian line.

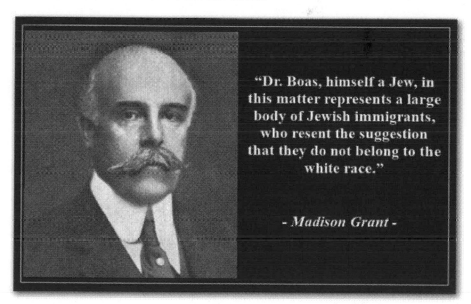

"Dr. Boas, himself a Jew, in this matter represents a large body of Jewish immigrants, who resent the suggestion that they do not belong to the white race."

- *Madison Grant* -

After World War II, in which the side that most overtly (and too extremely for most people's taste) represented eugenics, racial science and anti-Semitism was defeated, those ideas became widely discredited and perceived to be morally dangerous.

This, tragically, marked the final victory of Boasianism over Grantianism.

World War II was a war that all whites lost and that Jews, as a whole, won.

Of course that doesn't mean that whites went to war on behalf of the Jews, necessarily, although it can seem that way given the outcome. Rather, the war was caused by a series of diplomatic blunders, petty jealousies, power politics, clashing worldviews and – most significantly – the fallout and grievances carried over from World War I.

Though the Jewish role in this disaster should not be exaggerated, it should not be ignored, either. Their disproportionate role in the creation and propagation of Communism and the degeneracy of Weimar Germany; their influence over Western media; the outrageous Balfour Declaration and the handful of well-placed Jews in positions of power in Allied governments – notably in the FDR administration – all show them to have been an incredibly negative and disruptive force.

Thus the two lessons I believe should be drawn from WWII are 1) it was a brothers' war and all around tragedy that must never happen again and 2) the Jews are an alien people whose interests are invariably at odds with our own.

We cannot change the past. What we can do is accept the present for what it is and, to the best of our ability, look toward the future and forge a path that will lead us to eventual victory.

Counter-signalling our own grandfathers as having been tools of the Jew is idiotic and counterproductive, and something I want absolutely nothing to do with. Prior to Pearl Harbor the vast majority of the American public (80%-90%) were against intervention in the war.

They didn't know about the behind-the-scenes machinations of FDR, such as him deliberately provoking Japan and conspiring to circumvent the Neutrality Act with Churchill.* What they did know is that the Japs slaughtered their fellow countrymen in a brutal sneak attack and that four days later Hitler declared war on them.

What were they supposed to do after that, tuck tail and run?

Even the most prominent anti-war figure in the country, Charles Lindbergh, joined the war effort and selflessly did his patriotic duty after Pearl Harbor. He ended up flying a total of 50 combat missions in the Pacific Theater, never hesitating to face mortal danger head on, and developed an ingenious aircraft fuel saving technique.

There was much resistance to Lindbergh, who had resigned from the Army Air Corps two years earlier, getting involved in the war. His prior public opposition to FDR and the war and the slandering of his name in the media provoked questions of loyalty.

Between 1936 – 1938 Lindbergh had been sent by the U.S. government to Germany to evaluate their air combat capacity. While there he was awarded the Order of the German Eagle by Hitler and Goring. The Jews would later use this to attack him as a Nazi-

___
* See the Kent-Wolkoff affair.

sympathizing traitor. (He wasn't; he just refused to take a side in what he saw as an all around tragedy).

Lindbergh Accepts the Hitler Swastika From the Paws of the Monster Goering

Composographic Cartoon Conception by Roy L. Swann

TO HELL WITH LINDBERGH

DURING the World War there was in our House of Representatives a Congressman from Minnesota by the name of Charles A. Lindbergh. He was one of the foremost liberals of his day, even then advocating laws considered revolutionary to protect the free American worker and alleviate human misery. Some of them were passed years after his death. An immigrant, he knew the meaning of liberty. He fought tyranny. He never made a speech that would not have chained him to the rack in a concentration camp if he had lived in Germany today.

Congressman Lindbergh had a son whom he named after himself. The boy, a first generation American, was quick to take advantage of the inventive genius which has made this country great. He became a barnstorming flier with the instincts of a homing pigeon. Finally he made a flight which brought this Nation to its knees in adoration. Much greater flights have been made since, even by the Russians at whom he has sneered. He was the Nation's idol, the hero of American youth. He owed his fame to the opportunities which this Nation offered him.

Influential Americans took him in tow. He needed it. Our Ambassador Herrick in France told him to keep his mouth shut, the best advice a dumb hero can get, and saw to it that our Government brought the flier home for national acclaim. President Coolidge pinned him before the Nation, in the presence of the flier's mother who, for some reason, was not on speaking terms with her own son. Young Lindbergh received the Congressional Medal of Honor. He was made a Colonel. Bankers opened their arms to him and soon he was resting in them.

He became the glorified symbol for soaring aviation stocks and investors bought on the rise with the usual emotions. Later it was discovered that whatever goes up must come down, including Lindbergh. But his security was assured. It was inevitable that he should marry riches. Among newspapermen, whom he frequently insulted, he became an ubiquity. He began to vilenile on a high place. Even Alexis Carrel, distinguished scientist, took him under his wing. Lindbergh's household was ready to give him anything. But nobody is a hero to his valet and since Lindbergh has turned his back on a nation whose people he treats as valets let us look into his activities of recent months.

FIRST he bobs up in Moscow where he was honored and respected as a scientific aviator. Taking advantage of the hospitality of the warm-hearted Russians, who adore heroes and who treated him with extraordinary honor, this "has-been" flier returns to England, appears at a dinner given by Lady Astor and, at a critical time in world affairs, tells the Cliveden set, which sold out Czechoslovakia, that the Russian airfleet is in a chaotic condition. This was just what Hitler wanted.

For this "sell-out" he was branded as a liar by Russia's most famous aviators. They charged that in his aerial outings in Europe his favorite haunts were in Nazi Germany and that he was always the welcome guest of Herr Hitler and Field Marshal Goering—"a hanger-on and lackey

(Continued on Page 16)

What he concluded was that German air superiority was increasing rapidly. He recommended that the US build its own up to make itself untouchable, and then, in the spirit of our country's Founder, George Washington, stay out of any foreign conflict in which our vital interests are not at stake.

Lindbergh was an incredible man: he was a prolific author, aviator, military serviceman, archeologist, industrialist, inventor, explorer, political activist, scientist and racialist. He helped launch the space program. In 1927, he became the most famous and beloved person in the world after being the first to fly solo across the Atlantic ocean.

It's hard for us today to even imagine the excitement that must've been felt on the coast of Europe as Lindbergh's plane became visible above their shores, after 33 1/2 hours of the world waiting with bated breath not even knowing if he was dead or alive.

It was a world changing event. The dawning of a new age.

Upon his return to America, he was a celebrity to the point of having his life disrupted – something that he never wanted or asked for.

While he could've lived out his days in wealth and comfort and died as a hero to all, Lindbergh had a higher calling, which was to speak the truth as he saw it and stand up for what he thought was right no matter the consequences.

He joined with the America First Committee, which had been formed in 1940 to fight to keep the US out of the European conflict, and became its most visible and high-profile spokesman.

An estimated 150,000 people swarmed Lindbergh's plane, the Spirit of St. Louis, as he landed in Paris.

With his fame he drew breathtakingly large crowds and nonstop media attention, almost singlehandedly postponing US intervention until Pearl Harbor.

"I am advised to speak guardedly on the subject of the war," he once said to a crowd of 40,000 Americans gathered in Soldier Field.

> I am told that one must not stand too strongly against the trend of the times, and that, to be effective, what one says must meet with general approval. I prefer to say what I

71

believe, or not to speak at all. I would far rather have your respect for the sincerity of what I say, than attempt to win your applause by confining my discussion to popular concepts.

Lindbergh's bold determination to speak the truth at all costs finally led him to discussing the giant elephant in the room of US political life. In an infamous speech in Des Moines, Iowa, titled "Who Are the War Agitators," which was broadcast across the country via radio, Lindbergh bluntly called out the Jews as one of the main forces driving the country toward war.

"When this war started in Europe," he said

it was clear that the American people were solidly opposed to entering it. Why shouldn't we be? We had the best defensive position in the world; we had a tradition of independence from Europe; and the one time we did take part in a European war left European problems unsolved, and debts to America unpaid.

National polls showed that when England and France declared war on Germany, in 1939, less than 10 percent of our population favored a similar course for America. But there were various groups of people, here and abroad, whose interests and beliefs necessitated the involvement of the United States in the war. I shall point out some of these groups tonight, and outline their methods of procedure. In doing this, I must speak with the utmost frankness, for in order to counteract their efforts, we must know exactly who they are.

The three most important groups who have been pressing this country toward war are the British, the Jewish and the Roosevelt administration.

The "greatest danger" that the Jews posed to the US, he went on to say, "lies in their large ownership and influence in our motion pictures, our press, our radio and our government."

We cannot allow the natural passions and prejudices of other peoples to lead our country to destruction.

For daring to speak these obvious truths out loud, the Jews have viciously attacked this great man –

one of the most exemplary specimens our race has to offer – ever since.

For that alone they should be despised, and never forgiven.

The entire Jewish race isn't worth a fingernail of a Charles Lindbergh, so they should keep his name out of their filthy mouths.

As a fierce patriot Lindbergh's loyalty first and foremost was to America, but his concern was with the white race as a whole, which he was vehemently opposed to fighting *against*, but would gladly fight *with*.

An America First rally. **This** *is what we should desire to recreate, – not the Nuremberg Rally – and Trump has shown us that it is still possible.*

He stressed that "our bond with Europe is a bond of race and not of political ideology" and that

If the white race is ever seriously threatened,

74

it may then be time for us to take our part in its protection, to fight side by side with the English, French, and Germans, but not with one against the other for our mutual destruction.

When war finally did break out in Europe he wrote an article for Reader's Digest in which he pleaded for his fellow whites to come to their senses and warned that another intra-European conflict would only benefit the non-white and communist hordes and possibly even lead to the end of civilization itself.

"We, the heirs of European culture," he began

are on the verge of a disastrous war, a war within our own family of nations, a war which will reduce the strength and destroy the treasures of the White race, a war which may even lead to the end of our civilization.

[. . .]

Our civilization depends on a united strength among ourselves; on strength too great for foreign armies to challenge; on a Western Wall of race and arms which can hold back either a Genghis Khan or the infiltration of inferior blood; on an English fleet, a German air force, a French army, an American nation, standing together as guardians of our common heritage, sharing strength, dividing influence.

Our civilization depends on peace among

Western nations, and therefore on united strength, for Peace is a virgin who dare not show her face without Strength, her father, for protection. We can have peace and security only so long as we band together to preserve that most priceless possession, our inheritance of European blood, only so long as we guard ourselves against attack by foreign armies and dilution by foreign races.

[. . .]

With all the world around our borders, let us not commit racial suicide by internal conflict. We must learn from Athens and Sparta, before all of Greece is lost.

I don't know about you, fam, but I've never read a more moving statement in my life. It sends chills down my spine every time I read it.

This, I believe, should be the meme of our age:

Charles.

Lindbergh.

Was.

Right.

Why didn't we listen?

Europe was indeed decimated by the second World War, and half of it was handed over to the Communists afterward, just as Lindbergh had predicted would happen.

The Jews were not content with Nazi Germany

merely being conquered and bombed to rubble and its leaders being tried and executed. The most powerful Jew in America, Secretary of the Treasury under FDR, Henry Morgenthau, Jr., drew up a brutal, Old Testament-style Jewish revenge plan which called for Germany to be completely crushed and broken up into "several small, pastoral states of yeoman farmers."

Roosevelt, shockingly, signed off on the Morgenthau Plan until he was pressured by some of the more cool-headed gentiles in his administration, such as Secretary of War Henry Stimson (who called it "Semitism gone wild") to drop it.[*]

Stimson and others considered the main threat on the world stage to be communism and saw the rational course as building up Germany to act as a bulwark against the Soviet Union (which, it should be noted, Jews overwhelmingly supported prior to the early 1950s when Stalin began to turn on them).

One of America's most revered Generals, George S. Patton – the larger than life figure who was indispensable in winning the war – wanted to continue into Russia and roll over the Communist beast while we had the chance, to "finish the job now – while we are here and ready. . . . the Germans and the Poles hope to fight on our side soon."

Patton told Stimson's successor, Robert Patterson that the Soviet

---

[*] Richard Breitman, *FDR and the Jews*, 2013, p. 296

supply system is inadequate to maintain them in a serious action such as I could put to them. They have chickens in the coop and cattle on the hoof — that's their supply system. They could probably maintain themselves in the type of fighting I could give them for five days. After that it would make no difference how many million men they have, and if you wanted Moscow I could give it to you.

To not do this, he declared, would mean that we "have had a victory over the Germans and disarmed them, but we have failed in the liberation of Europe; we have lost the war!"

Upon coming in contact with European Jews in the Displaced Persons camps Patton was shocked, writing in his diary that they were "lost to all decency," the "greatest stinking bunch of humanity I have ever seen" and a "sub-human species without any of the cultural or social refinements of our time."[*]

He reported that they "refuse" to use toilets except as "repositories for tin cans, garbage, and refuse," instead "preferring to relieve themselves on the floor."

"The Jews," he explained, "were only forced to desist from their nastiness and clean up the mess by the threat of the butt end of rifles."

The smell of the Jews "was so terrible," wrote the battle-hardened man, whose nickname was Old

---

* See Martin Blumenson, *The Patton Papers: 1940-1945*, 1996

Blood and Guts, "that I almost fainted and actually about three hours later lost my lunch as the result of remembering it."

He concluded that the Jew is not "a human being" but is "lower than an animal."

We're not just going to shoot the bastards, we're going to cut out their living guts and use them to grease the treads of our tanks.

He viewed what was happening in occupied Germany as the "virus started by Morgenthau and

Baruch of a Semitic revenge" and against his "Anglo-Saxon conscience."

"I am frankly opposed to this war criminal stuff," he wrote to his loving wife, Beatrice, on September 14, 1945. "It is not cricket and is Semitic."

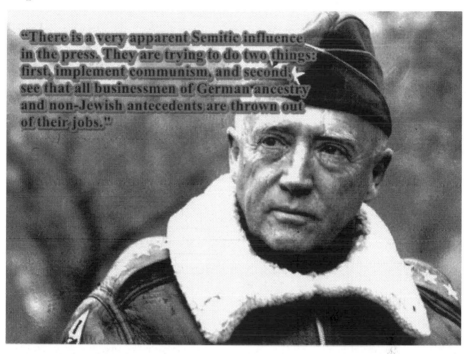

"There is a very apparent Semitic influence in the press. They are trying to do two things: first, implement communism, and second, see that all businessmen of German ancestry and non-Jewish antecedents are thrown out of their jobs."

Six weeks later he wrote her that "If what we are doing is 'Liberty, then give me death.' I can't see how Americans can sink so low. It is Semitic, and I am sure of it."

He decided to resign so he could come back to America and "tell the world a few truths which will be worth having."

"I hate to do it," he wrote, "but I have been gagged all my life, and whether they are appreciated or not, America needs some honest men who dare to say what they think, not what they think people want them to think."

Donald J. Trump ✔
@realDonaldTrump

"If everyone is thinking alike, then somebody isn't thinking."
--George S. Patton

♡ 1,802　2:30 PM - Nov 20, 2012

💬 1,692 people are talking about this

"I should not start a limited counter-attack, which would be contrary to my military theories," he wrote to a fellow officer, "but should wait until I can start an all out offensive."

It's very possible that he could've rode his immense popularity all the way into the White House.

It was for this reason, he suspected, that the "communist and semitic elements" in the press were hurling lies against him.

> In my opinion it is a deliberate attempt to alienate the soldier vote from the commanders because the communists know that soldiers are not communistic and they fear what eleven million votes [of veterans] would do.

He wrote to Beatrice that his resignation would be handed in "not later than Dec. 26," after which he would begin his "all out offensive."

Sadly, he would never get the chance. Five days before that date, on Dec. 21, he died in a military hospital from wounds he had sustained in a freak accident.

Thus our country and the world lost one of the greatest badasses of all time, and the enemies of civilization had not to deal with one of the only men who could've successfully stood up to them.

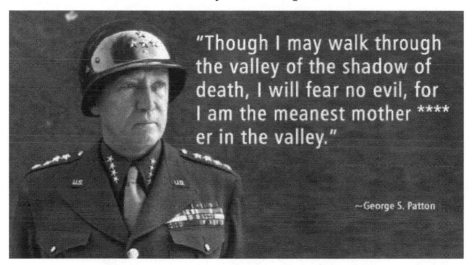

"Though I may walk through the valley of the shadow of death, I will fear no evil, for I am the meanest mother **** er in the valley."

~George S. Patton

It didn't take long for the wrath of the Jews to turn from Germany to the entire white world – their ancient, hated enemy – now with a renewed vigor since we 'didn't do enough to save them from Hitler.'

Jewish critic of Israel Norman Finkelstein wrote this about his tribe's attitude toward us:

> They're in an eternal war with all the goyim. All the goyim wanted the Jews dead. Just read Daniel Goldhagen ["Hitler's Willing Executioners"] if you have any doubts. The Americans are goyim. They refused entry to Jews fleeing the Holocaust; they didn't bomb the railway tracks to Auschwitz; they, too, wanted all the Jews dead. . . . Fuck the Americans! Fuck the goyim! Long live the

Jews!

With their control of the media and their newfound untouchable status as the world's foremost "victims," after the war the Jews proceeded to send western civilization into a hellish downward spiral that is rapidly leading to its destruction.

This perfect storm of unfortunate events culminated with the 1960s Jewish cultural revolution, which gained them almost complete control over every crucial element of American society.

It was at this time all of our defenses against the Jewish onslaught were broken down.

The 1924 Immigration Act was only overturned, after decades of Jewish lobbying efforts, in 1965. The "anti-miscegenation" and "one-drop" racial integrity laws were only fully overturned in 1967 by *Loving v. Virginia*, a case over the allowing of a racially mixed couple which was argued by (surprise!) a Jew, Bernard "Bernie" Cohen.

Obscenity laws, which held back the Jews' pornography, were strict until the mid-60s, after which they were drastically liberalized by cases initiated by Jewish activists and Jewish publishers (I wrote an entire book about this*).

Though it's hard not to become pessimistic and feel that America is too far gone to be saved, we must resist this urge. Those who try and gaslight us into adopting such an attitude should be avoided like the

* Benjamin Garland, *Merchants of Sin*, 2017

You feeling guilty enough yet, white man?

plague.

These same people will also argue that we as Americans don't have roots in the land, or that America was terminally liberal from the beginning.

To be consistent, those who argue that America is "too far gone" would have to say the same about just about all white countries, excluding maybe some in Eastern Europe such as Hungary and Poland.

In that case what would be the point of fighting at all? I guess we might as well just give up and accept our inevitable death.

In reality, America is still much more right wing than most other white nations. This was proven by the election of Trump, who ran on the most radically right wing platforms of any mainstream politician in many years.

Our very history, everything that millions of normal white Americans hold dear, is in itself offensive to the current neo-liberal order.

This is made abundantly clear as Trump is viciously attacked over appeals to basic American patriotism. When he adapted the motto "America First," he was connected to Lindbergh and the AFC, and by extension, anti-Semitism. The ADL tried to force him to apologize. He refused.

When he heaps praise upon Patton as having been a hero and one of our greatest generals, ditto.

Donald J. Trump @realDonaldTrump

"@Beyon: @oreillyfactor You know... DonaldTrump is looking pretty damn good as a presidential candidate. Maybe he is our modern day Patton?"

♡ 51   6:23 PM - Mar 31, 2015 · Manhattan, NY

♡ 37 people are talking about this

Even by putting up a picture of his favorite president, Andrew Jackson, Trump is roundly attacked by the media since, according to them, Jackson is to be condemned as an evil "dead white male" for his treatment of the Indians.

Normal white Americans agree with putting "America First," revere Charles Lindbergh, General Patton and Andrew Jackson and feel the attacks on Trump to be an attack on them, personally – and they are inspired by Trump's attitude of not ever backing down on issues such as these.

The significance of this simply cannot be overestimated.

There are millions of whites who would side with us – today – if only they had the leadership.

To help bring this leadership about, we must continue to do what we are doing: changing the culture. Supply will follow demand.

With the internet, we now have the power to create our own media and circumvent the Jewish filter.

All of their censorship efforts will ultimately fail, and will in fact strengthen us.

As long as we stay the course and don't allow our movement to devolve into something that is repulsive to the average person, slowly but surely, we will win more and more people to our side.

#NeverAgain

The majority of American whites are still conservative.

And they don't like the fact that they are being crowded out of their neighborhoods by non-whites or that they are subjected to daily doses of anti-white hate – that I can tell you.

Their natural racial feelings, if not explicit, are not far below the surface, and are only suppressed due to immense social pressure.

It's our job to educate these people and chip away any feelings of guilt they may have and instill in them a sense of pride over the history and achievements of their people.

And yes, we are now a distinct 'people' – a "new race," as Teddy Roosevelt explained in detail 130 years ago – forged by the taming of the wild frontier and the conquering of the savage Indian, and cut from the finest stock of Europe: the best of the best.

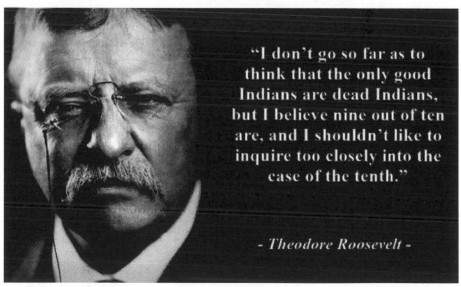

"I don't go so far as to think that the only good Indians are dead Indians, but I believe nine out of ten are, and I shouldn't like to inquire too closely into the case of the tenth."

- *Theodore Roosevelt* -

Nobody has done more to usher in the modern world than us.

The light bulb was invented by Americans.

The cellphone was invented by Americans.

GPS was invented by Americans.

The digital computer, personal computer, and finally the internet itself, were all invented by Americans.

It was Americans who enshrined freedom of speech into law, making it possible for me to speak these words to you on my American-invented computer and American-invented internet.

If I were in Europe, or many other parts of the world, I would probably be getting my door kicked in right about now.

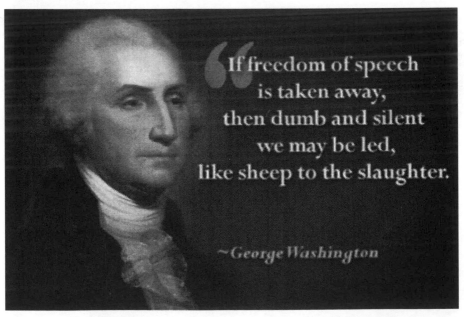

If freedom of speech is taken away, then dumb and silent we may be led, like sheep to the slaughter.

~George Washington

It was an American racialist and eugenicist,

William Shockley, who invented the transistor radio and founded Silicon Valley.

It was Americans – the Wright Brothers – who were the first in flight.

Henry Ford, the great American industrialist and anti-Semite, was the first to mass produce automobiles.

Americans went to the fucking moon.

To be American and alive right now is a blessing, for each and every one of us.

We have the opportunity, to an extent that surpasses most of those who came before us, to change the course of history for the better.

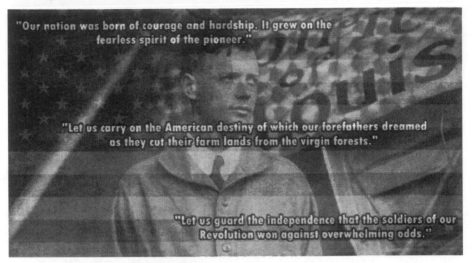

"Our nation was born of courage and hardship. It grew on the fearless spirit of the pioneer."

"Let us carry on the American destiny of which our forefathers dreamed as they cut their farm lands from the virgin forests."

"Let us guard the independence that the soldiers of our Revolution won against overwhelming odds."

Immortality awaits us.

Immortality for being the ones who stood firm against the forces of evil in our race's darkest hour.

Never forget that this country belongs to *us*.

We are its rightful inheritors.

And we will take it back.

We defeated tyranny in the past, and we'll do it again.

Because that's what Americans do.

Because the blood that flows in our veins demands nothing less.

Originally published on September 25, 2018

33782311R00057

Made in the USA
Middletown, DE
17 January 2019